the Cavalier King Charles Spaniel

A guide to selection, care, nutrition,

upbringing, training, health, breeding

sports and play.

Contents

Foreword

The book you are holding is a basic 'owners manual'
for everyone owning a Cavalier King Charles Spaniel
and also for those who are considering buying a
Cavalier King Charles Spaniel. What we have done in
this book is to give the information to help the (future)
owner of a Cavalier King Charles Spaniel look after his
or her pet responsibly. Too many people still buy a pet
before really understanding what they're about to get
into.

This book goes into the broad history of the Cavalier
King Charles Spaniel, the breed standard and some
pros and cons of buying a Cavalier. You will also find
essential information on feeding, initial training and
an introduction in reproduction. Finally we give attention to (day-to-day) care, health and some
breed-specific ailments.

Based on this information, you can buy a Cavalier
King Charles Spaniel, having thought it through carefully, and keep it as a pet in a responsible manner. Our
advice, though, is not just to leave it to this small book.
A properly brought-up and well-trained dog is more
than just a dog. Invest a little extra in a puppy training
course or an obedience course. There are also excellent
books available that go deeper into certain aspects than
is possible here.

About Pets

about pets

A Publication of About Pets.

Copyright © 2003
About Pets
co-publisher United Kingdom
Kingdom Books
PO9 5TL, England

ISBN 1852791853
First printing
September 2003

Original title: *de Cavalier*
King Charles spaniël
© 2001 - 2002 Welzo Media Productions bv,
About Pets bv
Warffum, the Netherlands
www.aboutpets.info

Photos:
Jos Dekker, D. de Moor, L. Haegens,
P. Jordens, Rob Dekker and
A.L.M. Zwaartman

Printed in Italy

In general

Together with the King Charles spaniel, the Cavalier is the smallest of the English spaniels.

With its eyes, with their look of constant surprise, and its alert nature it has a charming appearance, but just that may be its most dangerous pitfall. They have an extraordinary 'will to please', but are quickly distracted and their personality goes hand-in-hand with a large dose of 'joie de vivre'. As long as their owner enjoys a healthy sense of humour, he can follow various training courses with his Cavalier.

The Cavalier is an alert, slightly cocky companion, whereby many examples often still feel the instincts from the passion for hunting of their working ancestors flowing in their veins. That 'come!' response seems sometimes to be temporarily put on ice. Despite their 'innocent' little face, they

can be particularly tenacious in this respect. Their character is happy, sporty, affectionate, not aggressive, but should not show any tendency to nervousness and must certainly be fearless. The latter can sometimes be a problem if their soft nature is handled too harshly. Their mild nature ensures that they are not really difficult to bring up, but they have inherited that portion of cockiness essential to the spaniel family.

Though not anxious by nature, a Cavalier is soft hearted. In contrast to many small dogs, the Cavalier is all too aware of its diminutive build and will often act submissively (tail low, sometimes the whole hindquarters) towards other dogs (and people). This is easily confused with fear, but a frightened dog will never make a beeline for another dog (it would have to be crazy!).

It behaves well with other animals (dogs or not), but outdoors something running or flying away may well wake the hunting ancestry in it. This may extend your walk for an indefinite period until sir or madam decides it's time to return. Cavaliers may not be aggressive. An (aggressive) quick-tempered, pugnacious Cavalier is no Cavalier!

Origins

Various toy spaniels were to be found over the centuries at royal courts across Europe. They are often portrayed in paintings from the 16th, 17th and 18th centuries. This breed enjoyed its high point at the English court in the time of the Stuarts. Their popularity was at an all-time high during the reign of King Charles II. When the Dutch court took over, William III's favourite breed, the Pug, took over the crown. As the short snout then became fashionable, the long-snouted toy spaniel 'vanished' from the scene. Disappointed after a visit to England, where he failed to encounter a single living long-snouted toy spaniel, the American,

Rosswell Eldridge, started the initiative to breed this older type back again. For five years from 1927, he offered 25 pounds (at that time a princely sum) each year at Crufts for the example that most resembled those portrayed in paintings.

The club was founded in 1928 and the word 'Cavalier' added to the name to prevent confusion with the King Charles spaniel. It was only in 1945 that the British kennel club recognised the Cavalier.

Breed standard

A standard has been developed for all breeds recognised by the Kennel Club for the UK (and in Europe by the F.C.I. - the umbrella organisation for Western European kennel clubs). Officially approved kennel clubs in the member countries provide a translation. This standard provides a guideline for breeders and judges. It is something of an ideal that dogs of the breed must strive to match. With some breeds, dogs are already bred that match the ideal. Other breeds have a long way to go. There is a list of defects for each breed. These can be serious defects that disqualify the dog, and it will be excluded from breeding. Permitted defects are not serious, but do cost points in a show.

The UK Kennel Club breed standard for the Cavalier King Charles spaniel

General Appearance
Active, graceful and well balanced, with gentle expression.

Characteristics
Sporting, affectionate, absolutely fearless.

Temperament
Gay, friendly, non-aggressive; no tendency to nervousness.

Head and Skull
Skull almost flat between ears. Stop shallow. Length from base of stop to tip of nose about 3.8 cms (11/2 ins). Nostrils black and well developed without flesh marks, muzzle well tapered. Lips well developed but not pendulous. Face well filled below eyes. Any tendency to snipiness undesirable.

Eyes
Large, dark, round but not prominent; spaced well apart.

Ears
Long, set high, with plenty of feather.

Mouth
Jaws strong, with a perfect, regular and complete scissor bite, i.e. upper teeth closely overlapping lower teeth and set square to the jaws.

Neck
Moderate length, slightly arched.

Forequarters
Chest moderate, shoulders well laid back; straight legs moderately boned.

Body
Short-coupled with good spring of rib. Level back.

Hindquarters
Legs with moderate bone; well turned stifle – no tendency to cowhocks or sickle-hocks.

Feet
Compact, cushioned and well feathered.

Tail
Length of tail in balance with body, well set on, carried happily but never much above the level of the back. Docking optional. If docked, no more than one-third to be removed.

Gait/Movement
Free-moving and elegant in action, plenty of drive from behind. Forelegs and hindlegs move parallel when viewed from in front and behind.

Coat
Long, silky, free from curl. Slight wave permissible. Plenty of feathering. Totally free from trimming.

Colour
Recognised colours are:
Black and Tan: raven black with tan markings above the eyes, on cheeks, inside ears, on chest and legs and underside of tail. Tan should be bright. White marks undesirable.
Ruby: whole coloured rich red. White markings undesirable.
Blenheim: rich chestnut markings well broken up, on pearly white ground. Markings evenly divided on head, leaving room between ears for much valued lozenge mark or spot (a unique characteristic of the breed).
Tricolour: black and white well spaced, broken up, with tan markings over eyes, cheeks, inside ears, inside legs, and on underside of tail.
Any other colour or combination of colours highly undesirable.

Size
Weight: 5.4-8.2 kgs (12-18 lbs). A small, well balanced dog well within these weights desirable.

Faults
Any departure from the foregoing points should be considered a fault and the seriousness with which the fault should be regarded should be in exact proportion to its degree.

Note
Male animals should have two apparently normal testicles fully descended into the scrotum.
September 2000

Reproduced by courtesy of the Kennel Club of Great Britain

Buying a cavalier

Once you've made that properly considered decision to buy a dog, there are several options. Should it be a puppy, an adult dog, or even an older dog?

Should it be a bitch or dog, a pedigree dog or a cross? Of course, the question also comes up as to where to buy your dog - from a private person, a reliable breeder or an animal shelter? For you and the animal, it's vital to get these questions sorted out in advance. You want a dog that will fit your circumstances properly. With a puppy, you get a playful energetic housemate that will easily adapt to a new environment. If you want something quieter, an older dog is a good choice

The pros and cons of the Cavalier King Charles spaniel
They have inherited the friendly, happy and mild character of the spaniel family, but also a portion of cockiness and, to a greater or lesser extent, the passion for hun-

ting. It's therefore important to begin teaching them the 'come!' command at an early stage. Don't punish the dog if it responds too late, or not at all, otherwise you can forget the whole thing, and many Cavaliers are never let off the lead for that reason.

On the whole, the Cavalier is not difficult to train. But it is quickly distracted, so it's questionable whether it's suitable for dog sports at the highest level. Work is done with a Mediterranean touch. After all, one should not take life too seriously. That is something for other breeds. But some things are suitable for a Cavalier: obedience training, agility, flyball, doggy-dance, tracking and even hunt training, but all with tongue-in-cheek and one eye closed.

Its soft nature with its due portion of cockiness needs a rigorous, but certainly not harsh, upbringing. Many small breeds are very vigilant, and the Cavalier is no exception. Although some can be unusually frequent yappers, this has more to do with their upbringing than their nature. Their heart is too big to be watchdogs, there are better breeds for that. A cavalier will indeed bark, but once the burglar is inside it will lead him straight to the family jewels with its tail wagging.

The Cavalier knows that it's small. If you offer comfort or try to correct its humble or submissive behaviour towards other dogs, you can quickly wind up with a frightened, neurotic and withdrawn little dog. Keep your head up and keep walking as usual, ignoring its behaviour. It will grow out of it.

With too little attention (and walks) a Cavalier will quickly become dull and lethargic, which the breed does not deserve. Like all spaniels, the Cavalier also has

the **Cavalier King Charles Spaniel**

the tendency to easily get too fat, although they can be extremely fussy and generally poor eaters when they're young. Once they're past that stage, you need to watch their figure. The Cavalier also loses a lot of hair the whole year round, not just in the moulting season. It's amazing how much hair such a small animal can produce. Brushing every day won't stop this continuous moulting process, on the contrary! Because of its copious hair loss and the associated hair scale, the Cavalier is not really suitable for a family with asthma or allergies. It is important not to underestimate this to avoid serious problems in the future.

Furthermore, they remain spaniels. Once they've learned the pleasures of swimming, then they'll somehow manage to get into water on every walk, whatever the weather. The final point is seen by some as a disadvantage, others find it amusing: a Cavalier can snore with a passion.

Male or female?
Whether you choose a male or a female puppy, or an adult dog or

bitch, is an entirely personal decision. With the Cavalier, the difference in character between a male and a bitch is also not that great. Males are often reproached for urinating everywhere, being dominant, disobedient and running away, and for fidgeting with everything too. These problems are more to do with their upbringing than their nature. Admittedly, Cavaliers quickly become fidgets, but bitches do this too. You must naturally never tolerate this, however sweet it may look with a puppy. Bitches are often held to be more affectionate, but for a real cuddle you need to look among the males. The male is also somewhat more tolerant in nature. When a bitch has had enough, the male will lift his head and get up and go for the next round. Many males are more spontaneous and affectionate than bitches.
A male is usually more sturdy and ample in format. Naturally they want to set their own scent in places, but with your dog on the lead, you're in charge aren't you? And once they've set their first mark, their urgent need is taken care of. With a Cavalier, you also don't need to worry that it becomes too heavy to pull if necessary. You can also teach them to urinate only once or twice each time they go out on the lead.

A puppy test is good for defining the kind of character a young dog will develop. During a test one usually sees that a dog is more dominant than a bitch. You can often quickly recognise the bossy, the adventurous and the cautious characters. So visit the litter a couple of times early on. Try to pick a puppy that suits your own personality. A dominant dog, for instance, needs a strong hand. It will often try to see how far it can go. You must regularly make it clear who's the boss, and that it must obey all the members of the family.

When bitches are sexually mature, they will go into season. On average, a bitch is in season twice a year for about two or three weeks. This is the fertile period when she can become pregnant. Particularly in the second half of her season, she will want to go looking for a dog to mate with. A male dog will show more masculine traits once he is sexually mature. He will make sure other dogs know what territory is his by urinating as often as possible in as many places as he can. He is also difficult to restrain if there's a bitch in season nearby. As far as normal care is concerned there is little difference between a dog and a bitch.

Puppy or adult?

After you've made the decision for a male or female, the next question comes up. Should it be a puppy or an adult dog? Your household circumstances usually play a major role here.

Of course, it's great having a sweet little puppy in the house, but bringing up a young dog requires a lot of time. In the first year of its life it learns more than during the rest of its life. This is the period when the foundations are laid for elementary matters such as house-training, obedience and social behaviour. You must reckon with the fact that your puppy will keep you busy for a couple of hours a day, certainly in the first few months. You won't need so much time with a grown dog. It has already been brought up, but this doesn't mean it won't need correcting from time to time.

A puppy will no doubt leave a trail of destruction in its wake for the first few months. With a little bad luck, this will cost you a number of rolls of wallpaper, some good shoes and a few socks. In the worst case you'll be left with some chewed furniture. Some puppies even manage to tear curtains from their rails. With good upbringing this 'vandalism' will quickly disappear, but you won't have to worry about this if you get an older dog.

The greatest advantage of a puppy, of course, is that you can bring it up your own way. And the upbringing a dog gets (or doesn't get) is a major influence on its whole character. Finally, financial aspects may play a role in your choice. A puppy is generally (much) more expensive than an adult dog, not only in purchase price but also in 'maintenance'. A puppy needs to go to the vet's more often for the necessary vaccinations and check-ups.

Overall, bringing up a puppy requires a good deal of energy, time and money, but you have its upbringing in your own hands. An adult dog involves less money and time, but its character is already formed. You should also try to find out about the background of an adult dog. Its previous owner may have formed its character in somewhat less positive ways. In principle, Cavaliers are flexible dogs that will quickly get used to a new home, even at an old age.

Two dogs?

Having two or more dogs in the house is not just nice for us, but also for the animals themselves. Dogs get a lot of pleasure from their own company. After all, they are pack animals.

If you're sure that you want two young dogs, it's best not to buy them at the same time. Bringing a dog up and establishing the bond between dog and master takes time, and you need to give a lot of attention to your dog in this phase. Having two puppies in the house means you have to divide your attention between them. Apart from that, there's a danger that they will focus on one another

rather than on their master. Buy the second pup when the first is (almost) an adult.

Two adult dogs can happily be brought into the home together, as long as they're used to each other. If this is not the case, then they have to go through that process. This is usually best achieved by letting them get to know each other on neutral territory. This prevents fights for territory. On neutral territory, perhaps an acquaintance's garden where neither dog has been before, both dogs are basically equal. Once they've got to know each other, you can take them both home, and they can sort out the hierarchy there amongst themselves. In any event, don't get involved in trying to 'arbitrate'. That is human, but for the dog that's at the top of the pecking order it's like having its position undone. It will only make the dog more dominant in behaviour, with all the consequences. Once the hierarchy is established, most dogs can get along fine together.

Getting a puppy when the first dog is somewhat older often has a positive effect on the older dog. The influence of the puppy almost seems to give it a second childhood. The older dog, if it's been well brought up, can help with the up-bringing of the puppy. Young dogs like to imitate the behaviour of their elders. Don't forget to give both dogs the same amount of attention. Take both out alone at least once per day during the first eighteen months. Give the older dog enough opportunity to get some peace and quiet. It won't want an enthusiastic youngster running around under its feet all the time. Moreover, a puppy needs plenty of sleep and may have to have the brakes put on it once in a while.

The combination of a male and female needs special attention and, with the Cavalier too, it's good advice to get a second dog of the same sex. This will avoid a lot of problems. Sterilisation and castration is, of course, one solution, but it's a final one. A sterilised or castrated animal can never reproduce. However, sterilisation and castration can lead to abundant hair growth, which usually means a thicker, duller and stiffer coat that is difficult to groom.

A dog and children

Dogs and children are a great combination. They can play together and get great pleasure out of each other's company. Moreover, children need to learn how to handle living beings; they develop respect and a sense of responsibility by caring for a dog (or other pets). However sweet a dog is, children must understand that it is an animal and not a toy. A dog isn't comfortable when it's being messed around with. It can become frightened, timid and even aggressive. So make it clear what a dog likes and what it doesn't. With the Cavalier, it's important to make sure the dog doesn't allow too much. Look for ways the child can play with the dog, perhaps a game of hide and seek where the child hides and the dog has to find it. Even a simple tennis ball can give enormous pleasure. Children must learn to leave a dog in peace when it doesn't want to play any more. The dog must also have its own place where it's not disturbed. Have children help with your dog's care as much as possible. A strong bond will be the result.

The arrival of a baby also means changes in the life of a dog. Before the birth you can help get the dog acquainted with the new situation. Let it sniff at the new things in the house and it will quickly accept them. When the baby has arrived involve the dog as much as possible in day-by-day events, but make sure it gets plenty of attention too. NEVER leave a dog alone with young children. Crawling infants sometimes make unexpected movements, which can easily frighten a dog. And infants are hugely curious, and may try to find out whether the tail is really fastened to the dog, or whether its eyes come out, just like they do with their cuddly toys. But a dog is a dog and it will defend itself when it feels threatened.

Where to buy

There are various ways of acquiring a dog. The decision for a puppy or an adult dog will also define for the most part where to buy your dog.

If it's to be a puppy, then you need to find a breeder with a litter. If you chose a popular breed like the Cavalier there is choice enough. But you may also face the problem that there are so many puppies on sale that have only been bred for profit's sake. You can see how many puppies are for sale by looking in the regional newspaper every Saturday. Some of these dogs have a pedigree, but many don't. These breeders often don't watch out for breed-specific illnesses and in-breeding; puppies are separated from their mother as fast as possible and are thus insuf-ficiently socialised. Never buy a puppy that is too young, or whose mother you weren't able to see.

Fortunately there are also enough bona-fide breeders of Cavaliers. Try to visit a number of breeders before you actually buy your puppy. Ask if the breeder is prepared to help you after you've bought your puppy, and to help you find solutions for any problems that may come up.

If you're looking for an adult dog, it's best to contact the breed asso-ciation, who often help place adult

dogs that can no longer be kept by their owners because of personal circumstances (impulse buying, moving home, divorce etc.).

Things to watch out for

Buying a puppy is no simple matter. You must pay attention to the following:

• Never buy a puppy on impulse, even if it is love at first sight. A dog is a living being that will need care and attention over a long period. It is not a toy that you can put away when you're finished with it.

• Take a good look at the mother. Is she calm, nervous, aggressive, well cared-for or neglected? The behaviour and condition of the mother is not only a sign of the quality of the breeder, but also of the puppy you're about to buy.

• Avoid buying a puppy whose mother has been kept only in a kennel. A young dog needs as many different impressions as possible in its first few months, including living in a family group. It gets used to people and possibly other pets. Kennel dogs miss these experiences and are inadequately socialised. Always ask to see the parents' papers (vaccination certificates, pedigrees, official reports of health examinations).

• Never buy a puppy younger than eight weeks.

• Put all agreements with the breeder in writing. A model agreement is available from the breed association.

Finally, you must realise that a pedigree is nothing more or less than a proof of descent. The kennel club also issues pedigrees to the young of parents that suffer from a congenital condition, or that have never been checked for them. A pedigree says nothing about the health of the parent dogs or of your puppy.

Ten golden puppy rules

1. Walk your puppy in doses followed by one hour play, a feed and then three hours sleep.
2. Don't let your puppy run endlessly after a ball or stick.
3. Don't let your puppy romp wildly with large, heavy dogs.
4. Never let your puppy play on a full tummy.
5. Don't give your puppy anything to drink straight after a meal.
6. Don't let your puppy walk up and down steps for the first year. Be careful with shiny floors.
7. Don't add supplements to ready-made food.
8. Watch out for your puppy's weight. Being overweight can lead to bone abnormalities.
9. Give your puppy a quiet place to sleep.
10. Pick your puppy up carefully, one hand under its chest, the other under its hindquarters.

Travelling with your Cavalier

There are a few things to think about before travelling with your dog. While one dog may enjoy travelling, another may hate it. You may like holidays in far-away places, but it's questionable whether your dog will enjoy them as much.

That very first trip

The first trip of a puppy's life is also the most nerve-wracking. This is the trip from the breeder's to its new home. If possible, pick up your puppy in the morning. It then has the whole day to get used to the new situation. Ask the breder not to feed it that day. The young animal will be overwhelmed by all kinds of new experiences. Firstly, it's away from its mother; it's in a small room (the car) with all its different smells, noises and strange people. So there's a big chance that the puppy will be car-sick this first time, with the annoying consequence that it will remember travelling in the car as an unpleasant experience.

So it's important to make this first trip as pleasant as possible. When picking up a puppy, always take someone with you who can sit in the back seat with the puppy on his or her lap and talk to it calmly. If it's too warm for the puppy, a place on the floor at the feet of your companion is ideal. The pup will lie there relatively quietly and may even take a nap. Ask the breeder for a cloth or something else from the puppies basket or bed that carries a familiar scent. The puppy can lie on this in the car, and it will also help if it feels lonely during the first nights at home.

If the trip home is a long one, then stop for a break (once in a while). Let your puppy roam and sniff around (on the lead!), offer it a little drink and, if necessary, do its business. Do take care to lay an old towel in the car. It can happen that the puppy, in its nervousness, may urinate or be sick. It's also good advice to give a puppy positive experiences with car journeys. Make short trips to nice places where you can walk and play with it. It can be a real nuisance if your dog doesn't like travelling in a car. After all, once in a while you will have to take it to certain places, such as the vet's or to visit friends and acquaintances.

Taking your Cavalier on holiday

When making holiday plans, you also need to think about what you-'re going to do with your dog during that time. Are you taking it with you, putting it into kennels or leaving it with friends? In any event there are a number of things you need to do in good time. If you want to take your dog with you, you need to be sure in advance that it will be welcome at your holiday home, and what rules there are. If you're going abroad it will need certain vaccinations and a health certificate, which normally need to be done four weeks before departure. You must also be sure that you've made all the arrangements necessary to bring your dog back home to the UK, without it needing to go into quarantine under the rabies regulations. Your vet can give you the most recent information.

If your trip is to southern Europe, ask for a treatment against ticks

(you can read more about this in the chapter on parasites).

Although dog-owners usually enjoy taking their dog on holiday, you must seriously ask yourself whether the dog feels that way too. Cavaliers certainly don't always feel comfortable in a hot country. Days spent travelling in a car are also often not their preference, especially if they suffer badly from car-sickness. There are good medicines for this, but it's questionable whether you're doing your dog a favour with them. If you do decide to take it with you, make regular stops at safe places during your journey, so that your dog can have a good run. Take plenty of fresh drinking water with you, as well as the food your dog is used to. Don't leave your dog in the car standing in the sun. It can quickly be overcome by the heat, with even fatal consequences. If you can't avoid it, park the car in the shade if at all possible, and leave a window open for a little fresh air. Even if you've taken these precautions, never stay away long!

If you're travelling by plane or ship, make sure in good time that your dog can travel with you and what rules you need to observe. You will need some time to make all the arrangements. Maybe you decide not to take your dog with you, and you then need to find somewhere for it to stay.

Arrangements for a place in kennels need to be made well in advance, and there may be certain vaccinations required, which need to be given a minimum of one month before the stay.
If your dog can't be accommodated in the homes of relatives or friends, it might be possible to have an acquaintance stay in your house. This also needs to be arranged well in advance, as it may be difficult to find someone who can do this.

Always ensure that your dog can be traced should it run away or get lost while on holiday. A little tube with your address or a tag with home and holiday address can avoid a lot of problems.

Moving home

Dogs generally become more atta-
ched to humans than to the house
they live in. Moving home is usually not a problem for them. But it
can be useful before moving to let
the dog get to know its new home
and the area around it.

If you can, leave your dog with
relatives or friends (or in kennels)
on the day of the move. The chance of it running away or getting
lost is then practically non-
existent. When your move is complete, you can pick your up dog
and let it quietly get familiar with
its new home and environment.
Give it its own place in the house
at once and it will quickly adapt.
During the first week or so, always
walk your dog on a lead because
an animal can also get lost in new
surroundings. Always take a different route so it quickly gets to
know the neighbourhood.

Don't forget to get your new
address and phone number engra-
ved on the dog's tag. Send a change of address notice to the chip or
tattoo registration office. Dogs
must sometimes be registered in a
new community.

Feeding
your Cavalie

A dog will eat a lot more than just meat. In the wild it would eat its prey complete with skin and fur, including the bones, stomach, and the innards with their semi-digested vegetable material.

In this way the dog supplements its meat menu with the vitamins and minerals it needs. This is also the basis for feeding a domestic dog.

Ready-made foods

It's not easy for a layman to put together a complete menu for a dog, that includes all the necessary proteins, fats, vitamins and minerals in just the right proportions and quantities. Meat alone is certainly not a complete meal for a dog. It contains too little calcium. A calcium deficiency over time will lead to bone defects, and for a fast-growing puppy this can lead to serious skeletal deformities.

If you mix its food yourself, you can easily give your dog too much in terms of vitamins and minerals, which can also be bad for your

dog's health. You can avoid these problems by giving it ready-made food of a good brand. These products are well-balanced and contain everything your dog needs. Supplements such as vitamin preparations are superfluous. The amount of food your dog needs depends on its weight and activity level. You can find guidelines on the packaging. Split the food into two meals per day if possible, and always ensure there's a dish of fresh drinking water next to its food.

Give your dog the time to digest its food, don't let it outside straight after a meal. A dog should also never play on a full stomach. This can cause stomach torsion, (the stomach turning over), which can be fatal for your dog.

Because the nutritional needs of a dog depend, among other things, on its age and way of life, there are many different types of dog food available. There are "light" foods for less active dogs, "energy" foods for working dogs and "senior" foods for the older dog.

Canned foods, mixer and dry foods

Ready-made foods available at pet shops or in the supermarket can roughly be split into canned food, mixer and dry food. Whichever form you choose, ensure that it's a complete food with all the necessary ingredients. You can see this on the packaging.

Most dogs love canned food. Although the better brands are composed well, they do have one disadvantage: they are soft. A dog fed only on canned food will sooner or later have problems with its teeth (plaque, paradontosis). Besides canned food, give your dog hard foods at certain times or a dog chew, such as Nylabone Healthy Edibles.

Mixer is a food consisting of chunks, dried vegetables and grains. Almost all moisture has been extracted. The advantages of mixer are that it is light and keeps well. You add a certain amount of water and the meal is ready. A disadvantage is that it must definitely not be fed without water. Without the extra fluid, mixer will

absorb the fluids present in the stomach, with serious results. Should your dog manage to get at the bag and enjoy its contents, you must immediately give it plenty to drink.

Dry chunks have also had the moisture extracted but not as much as mixer. The advantage of dry foods is that they are hard, forcing the dog to use its jaws, removing plaque and massaging the gums.

Dog chew products

Of course, once in a while you want to spoil your dog with something extra. Don't give it pieces of cheese or sausage as these contain too much salt and fat. There are various products available that a dog will find delicious and which are also healthy, especially for its teeth, such as Nylabone. You'll find a large range of varying quality in the pet shop.

The butcher's left-overs
The bones of slaughtered animals have traditionally been given to the dog, and dogs love them, but they are not without risks. Pork and poultry bones are too weak. They can splinter and cause serious injury to the intestines. Beef bones are more suitable, but they must first be cooked to kill off dangerous bacteria.
Pet shops carry a range of smoked, cooked and dried abattoir residue, such as pigs' ears, bull

penis, tripe sticks, oxtails, gullet, dried muscle meat, and hoof chews.

Fresh meat

If you do want to give your dog fresh meat occasionally, never give it raw, but always boiled or roasted. Raw (or not fully cooked) pork or chicken can contain life-threatening bacteria.

Chicken can be contaminated by the notorious salmonella bacteria, while pork can carry the Aujeszky virus. This disease is incurable and will quickly lead to the death of your pet.

Buffalo or cowhide chews

Dog chews are mostly made of beef or buffalo hide. Chews are usually knotted or pressed hide and can come in the form of little shoes, twisted sticks, lollies, balls and various other shapes; nice to look at and a nice change.

Munchy sticks

Munchy sticks are green, yellow, red or brown coloured sticks of various thicknesses. They consist of ground buffalo hide with a number of often-undefined additives. The composition and quality of these between-meal treats is not

information you should keep in mind. Dogs that get too fat are often given too much food or treats between meals. Gluttony or boredom can also be a cause, and a dog often puts on weight following castration or sterilisation. Due to changes in hormone levels it becomes less active and consumes less energy. Finally, simply too little exercise alone can lead to a dog becoming overweight.

You can use the following rule of thumb to check whether your dog is overweight: you should be able to feel its ribs, but not see them. If you can't feel its ribs then your dog is much too fat. Overweight dogs live a passive life, they play too little and tire quickly. They also suffer from all kinds of medical problems (problems in joints and heart conditions). They usually die younger too.

always clear. Some are fine, but there have also been sticks found to contain high levels of cardboard and even paint residues. Choose a product whose ingredients are clearly described.

Overweight?

Recent investigations have shown that many dogs are overweight. A dog usually gets too fat because of over-feeding and lack of exercise. Use of medicines or a disease is rarely the cause. Cavaliers have a tendency to quickly get fat, so they need less than you might expect for their size, a piece of

So it's important to make sure your dog doesn't get too fat. Always follow the guidelines on food packaging. Adapt them if your dog is less active or gets lots of snacks. Try to make sure your dog gets plenty of exercise by playing and running with it as much as you can. If your dog starts to show signs of putting on weight you can switch to a low-calorie food. If it's really too fat and reducing its food quantity doesn't help, then a special diet is the only solution.

Caring for your Cavalie

Good (daily) care is extremely important for your dog. A well cared for dog is less likely to become ill.

Caring for your dog is not only necessary but also a pleasure. Master and dog are giving each other some attention, and it's an excellent opportunity for a game and a cuddle.

The coat

Caring for your dog's coat involves regular brushing and combing, together with checking for parasites such as fleas, mites or ticks. How often a dog needs to be brushed and combed depends on its type of coat. Brushing removes dead hairs and irregularities and spreads body fat throughout the whole coat. Check your Cavalier daily, especially when it's moulting, for tangles behind the ear, in its groin and breech. These are best removed by brushing them out. The tangles usually fall out and you don't need get the scissors out.

Brush your dog thoroughly twice a week. First free up the coat with a stiff brush (rigorously like a massage), then comb it until all irregularities are gone. After that, brush it again with a soft brush to spread the fat. On a Cavalier, some long, dead or dull hair will stay behind, especially on the skull. You can remove these by carefully plucking them out in the direction of the coat, while holding the spot where they need to come out with your other hand. Removing this hair makes room for new hair to grow. Moulting can irritate the dog and removing this old fur will provide relief. Use the right equipment for taking care of the coat. A stiff brush, a soft-haired brush, a rubber brush a medium-fine comb and a fine flea brush (preferably not plastic). Combs should not be too sharp. Always comb from the head back towards the tail, following the direction of the hair.

Superfluous hair between the soles of the feet should be kept short. This is more pleasant for the dog, otherwise it 'slides' on these and collects particles of soil and dirt making walking unpleasant.

If you get a puppy used to being brushed from an early age, it will enjoy having its coat cared for. Only bathe a dog when it's necessary. Always use a special dog shampoo and make sure it doesn't get into the dog's eyes or ears. Rinse the suds out thoroughly. A vet can prescribe special medicinal shampoos for some skin conditions. Always follow the instructions to the letter. Make sure your Cavalier is completely dry before letting it outdoors again. Even dogs can catch a cold!

Good flea prevention is highly important to avoid skin and coat problems. Fleas must be treated not only on the dog itself but also in its surroundings (see the chapter on parasites). Coat problems can also occur due to an allergy to certain food substances. In such cases, a vet can prescribe a hypo-allergenic diet.

Teeth

A dog must be able to eat properly to stay in good condition, so it needs healthy teeth. Check its teeth regularly. Get in touch with your vet if you suspect that all is not well. Regular feeds of hard dry food can help keep your dogs teeth clean and healthy. There are special dog chews, such as Nylabone, on the market that help prevent plaque and help keep the animal's breath fresh.

What really helps is regular tooth-brushing. You can use special tooth-brushes for dogs, but a finger wrapped in a small piece of gauze will also do the job. Get your dog used to having its teeth cleaned at an early age and you won't have problems.

You can even teach an older dog to have its teeth cleaned. With a dog chew as a reward it will certainly be happy.

Nails

On a dog that regularly walks on hard surfaces, its nails usually grind themselves down. In this case there's no need to clip their nails. But it wouldn't do any harm to check their length now and again, especially on dogs that don't get out on the streets often. Using a piece of paper, you can easily see whether its nails are too long. If you can push the paper between the nail and the ground when the dog is standing, then the

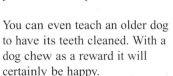

nail is the right length.
Nails that are too long can bother
a dog. It can injure itself when
scratching, so they must be kept
trimmed. You can buy special nail
clippers in pet shops. Be careful
not to clip back too far as you
could damage the skin around the
nail, which can bleed profusely. If
you feel unsure, have this necessary task done by a vet or an animal
beauty parlour.

Special attention is needed for the
dewclaw, this being the nail on the
inside of the hind leg. Clip this nail
back regularly, otherwise it can get
caught on it and become damaged.

Eyes

A dog's eyes should be cleaned
regularly. Discharge gets into the
corners of the eye. You can easily
remove them by wiping them
downward with your thumb. If
you don't like doing that, use a
piece of tissue or toilet paper.

Keeping your dog's eyes clean
will take only a few seconds a
day, so do it every day. If the discharge becomes yellow this could
point to an irritation or infection.
Eye drops (from your vet) will
quickly solve this problem.

Ears

The ears are often forgotten when
caring for dogs, but they must be
checked at least once a week. If
its ears are very dirty or have too
much wax, you must clean them.

This should preferably be done
with a clean cotton cloth, moistened with lukewarm water or baby
oil. Cotton wool is not suitable
due to the fluff it can leave
behind. NEVER penetrate the ear
canal with an object.

If hairs inside the ears cause problems, then it's better to remove
them. Carefully pull them out
using your thumb and index finger.

If you do neglect cleaning your
dog's ears there's a substantial risk
of infection. A dog that is constantly scratching at its ears might
be suffering from dirty ears, an
ear infection or ear mites, making
a visit to the vet essential.

Bringing up your Cavalie

It is very important that your dog is properly brought up and is obedient. Not only will this bring you more pleasure, but it's also nicer for your environment.

A puppy can learn what it may and may not do by playing. Rewards and consistency are important tools in bringing up a dog. Reward it with your voice, a stroke or something tasty and it will quickly learn to obey. A puppy-training course can also help you along the way.

(Dis)obedience

A dog that won't obey you is not just a problem for you, but also for your surroundings. It's therefore important to avoid unwanted behaviour. In fact, this is what training your dog is all about, so get started early. 'Start 'em young!' applies to dogs too. An untrained dog is not just a nuisance, but can also cause dangerous situations, running into the road, chasing joggers or jumping at

people. A dog must be trained out of this undesirable behaviour as quickly as possible. The longer you let it go on, the more difficult it will become to correct. The best thing to do is to attend a special obedience course. This won't only help to correct the dog's behaviour, but its owner also learns how to handle undesirable behaviour at home. A dog must not only obey its master during training, but at home too.

Always be consistent when training good behaviour and correcting annoying behaviour. This means a dog may always behave in a certain way, or must never behave that way. Reward it for good behaviour and never punish it after the fact for any wrongdoing. If your dog finally comes after you've been calling it a long time, then reward it. If you're angry because you had to wait so long, it may feel it's actually being punished for coming. It will probably not obey at all the next time for fear of punishment.

Try to take no notice of undesirable behaviour. Your dog will perceive your reaction (even a negative one) as a reward for this behaviour. If you need to correct the dog, then do this immediately. Use your voice or grip it by the scruff of its neck and push it to the ground. This is the way a mother dog calls her pups to order. Rewards for good behaviour are, by far, preferable to punishment; they always get a better result.

House-training
The very first training (and one of the most important) that a dog needs is house-training. The basis for good house-training is keeping a good eye on your puppy. If you pay attention, you will notice that it will sniff a long time and turns around a certain spot before doing its business there. Pick it up gently and place it outside, always at the same place. Reward it abundantly if it does its business there.

Another good moment for house-training is after eating or sleeping. A puppy often needs to do its business at these times. Let it relieve itself before playing with it, other-wise it will forget to do so and you'll not reach your goal. For the first few days, take your puppy out for a walk just after it's eaten or woken up. It will quickly learn the meaning, especially if it's rewarded with a dog biscuit for a successful attempt. Of course, it's not always possible to go out after every snack or snooze. Lay newspapers at different spots in the house. Whenever the pup needs to do its business, place it on a newspaper. After some time it will start to look for a place itself. Then start to reduce the number of newspapers until there is just one left, at the front or back door. The puppy will learn to go to the door if it needs to relieve itself.

Then you put it on the lead and go out with it. Finally you can remove the last newspaper. Your puppy is now house-trained.

One thing that certainly won't work is punishing an accident after the fact. A dog whose nose is rubbed in its urine or its droppings won't understand that at all. It will only get frightened of you. Rewarding works much better than punishment. An indoor kennel or cage can be a good tool in helping with house-training. A puppy won't foul its own nest, so a kennel can be a good solution for the night, or during periods in the day when you can't watch it. But a kennel must not become a prison where your dog is locked up day and night.

Basic Obedience

The basic commands for an obedient dog are those for sit, lie down, come and stay. But a puppy should first learn its name. Use the puppies name as much as possible from the first day on followed by a friendly 'Come!' Reward it with your voice and a stroke when it comes to you. Your puppy will quickly recognise the intention and has now learned its first command in a playful manner. Don't appear too strict towards a young puppy, and don't always punish it immediately if it doesn't always react in the right way. When you call your puppy to you in this way have it come right to

you. You can teach a pup to sit by holding a piece of dog biscuit above its nose and then slowly moving it backwards. The puppy's head will also move backwards until its hind legs slowly go down. At that moment you say 'Sit!' After a few attempts, it will quickly know this nice game. Use the 'Sit!' command before you give your dog its food, put it on the lead, or before it's allowed to cross the street.

Teaching the command to lie down is similar. Instead of moving the piece of dog biscuit backwards, move it down vertically until your hand reaches the ground and then forwards. The dog will also move its forepaws forwards and lie down on its own. At that moment say 'Lie down!' This command is useful when you want a dog to be quiet.

Two people are needed for the 'Come!' command. One holds the dog back while the other runs away. After about fifteen metres, he stops and enthusiastically says 'Come!' The other person now lets the dog go, and it should obey the command at once. Again you reward it abundantly. The 'Come!' command is useful in many situations and good for safety too. This is a particularly important command for the Cavalier, otherwise your companion may be condemned to always being walked on the lead.

A dog learns to stay from the sitting or lying position. While its sitting or lying down, you give the command: 'Stay!' and then step back one step. If the dog moves with you, quietly put it back in position, without displaying anger. If you do react angrily, you're actually punishing it for coming to you, and you'll only confuse your dog. It can't understand that coming is rewarded one time, and punished another. Once the dog stays nicely, reward it abundantly. Practice this exercise with increasing distances (at first no more than one metre). The 'Stay!' command is useful when getting out of the car.

Courses

Obedience courses to help you bring up your dog are available across the country. These courses are not just informative, but also fun for dog and master.

With a puppy, you can begin with a puppy course. This is designed to provide the basic training.

A puppy that has attended such a course has learned about all kinds of things that will confront it in later life: other dogs, humans, traffic and what these mean. The puppy will also learn obedience and to follow a number of basic commands. Apart from all that, attention will be given to important subjects such as brushing, being alone, travelling in a car, and doing its business in the right places.

The next step after a puppy course is a course for young dogs. This course repeats the basic exercises and ensures that the growing dog doesn't learn bad habits. After this, the dog can move on to an obedience course for full-grown dogs. For more information on where to find courses in your area, contact your local kennel club. You can get its address from the Kennel Club of Great Britain in London. In some areas, the RSPCA organises obedience classes and your local branch may be able to give you information.

Play and toys
There are various ways to play with your dog, You can romp and run with it, but also play a number of games, such as retrieving, tug-of-war, hide-and-seek and catch. A tennis ball is ideal for retrieving, you can play tug-of-war with an old sock or a special tugging rope. Start with tug-of-war only when your dog is a year old.

A puppy must first get its second teeth and then they need several months to strengthen. There's a real chance of your dog's teeth becoming deformed if you start too young. You can use almost anything for a game of hide-and-seek. A frisbee is ideal for catching games. Never use too small a ball for games. It can easily get lodged into the dog's throat.

Play is extremely important. Not only does it strengthen the bond between dog and master, but it's also healthy for both. Make sure that you're the one that ends the game. Only stop when the dog has brought back the ball or frisbee, and make sure you always win the tug-of-war. This confirms your dominant position in the hierarchy. Use these toys only during play so that the dog doesn't forget their significance. When choosing a special dog toy, remember that dogs are hardly careful with them. So always buy toys of good quality that a dog can't easily destroy.

Be very careful with sticks and twigs. The latter, particularly, can easily splinter. A splinter of wood in your dog's throat or intestines can cause awful problems. Throwing sticks or twigs can also be dangerous. If they stick into the ground a dog can easily run into them with an open mouth.

If you would like to do more than just play games, you can now also play sports with your dog. For people who want to do more, there are various other sporting alternatives such as Flyball, Agility and Obedience.

Aggression

Cavaliers should never appear aggressive. But even they can sometimes be difficult with other animals or people, so it's good to understand more about the background of aggression in dogs.

There are two different types of aggressive behaviour: The anxious-aggressive dog and the dominant-aggressive dog. An anxious-aggressive dog can be recognised by its pulled back ears and its low position. It will have pulled in its lips, showing its teeth. This dog is aggressive because it's very frightened and feels cornered. It would prefer to run away, but if it can't then it will bite to defend itself. It will grab its victim anywhere it can. The attack is usually brief and, as soon as the dog can see a way to escape, it's gone. In a confrontation with other dogs, it will normally turn out as the loser. It can become even more aggressive once it's realised that people or other dogs are afraid of it. This behaviour cannot be corrected just like that. First you have to try and understand what the dog is afraid of. Professional advice is a good idea here because the wrong approach can easily make the problem worse.

The dominant-aggressive dog's body talk is different. Its ears stand up and its tail is raised and stiff. This dog will always go for its victim's arms, legs or throat. It is extremely self-assured and highly placed in the dog hierarchy. Its attack is a display of power rather than a consequence of fear. This dog needs to know who's boss. You must bring it up rigorously and with a strong hand. An obedience course can help.

A dog may also bite itself because it's in pain. This is a natural defensive reaction. In this case try to resolve the dog's fear as far as possible. Reward him for letting you get to the painful spot. Be careful, because a dog in pain may also bite its master! Muzzling it can help prevent problems if you have to do something that may be painful. Never punish a dog for this type of aggression!

Fear

The source of anxious behaviour can often be traced to the first weeks of a dog's life. A shortage of new experiences during this important phase (also called the 'socialisation phase') has great influence on its later behaviour. A dog that never encountered humans, other dogs or animals during the socialisation phase will be afraid of them later. This fear is common in dogs brought up in a barn or kennel, with almost no contact with humans. As we saw,

fear can lead to aggressive behaviour, so it's important that a puppy gets as many new impressions as possible in the first weeks of its life. Take it with you into town in the car or on the bus, walk it down busy streets and allow it to have plenty of contact with people, other dogs and other animals.

It's a huge task to turn an anxious, poorly socialised dog into a real pet. It will probably take an enormous amount of attention, love, patience and energy to get such an animal used to everything around it. Reward it often and give it plenty of time to adapt and, over time, it will learn to trust you and become less anxious. Try not to

force anything, because that will always have the reverse effect. Here too, an obedience course can help a lot. A dog can be especially afraid of strangers. Have visitors give it something tasty as a treat. Put a can of dog biscuits by the door so that your visitors can spoil your dog when they arrive. Here again, don't try to force anything. If the dog is still frightened, leave it in peace.

Dogs are often frightened in certain situations; well-known examples are thunderstorms and fireworks. In these cases try to ignore their anxious behaviour. If you react to their whimpering and whining, it's the same as rewarding it. If you ignore its fear completely, the dog will quickly learn that nothing is wrong. You can speed up this 'learning process' by rewarding its positive behaviour.

Rewarding

Rewarding forms the basis for bringing up a dog. Rewarding good behaviour works far better than punishing bad behaviour and rewarding is also much more fun. Recently the opinions on upbringing for dogs have gradually changed. In the past the proper way to correct bad behaviour was a sharp pull on the lead. Today, experts regard rewards as a positive incentive to get dogs to do what we expect of them. There are many ways to reward a dog. The usual ways are a stroke or a friendly word, even without a tasty treat to go with it. Of course, a piece of dog biscuit does wonders when you're training a puppy. Be sure you always have something delicious in your pocket to reward good behaviour. Another form of reward is play. Whenever a dog notices you have a ball in your pocket, it won't go far from your side. As soon as you've finished playing, put the ball away. This way your dog will always do its best in exchange for a game.

Despite the emphasis you put on rewarding good behaviour, a dog can sometimes be a nuisance or disobedient. You must correct such behaviour immediately. Always be consistent: once 'no', always 'no'.

Barking

Dogs which bark too much and too are often a nuisance for their surroundings. A dog-owner may tolerate barking up to a point, but neighbours are often annoyed by the unnecessary noise. Don't encourage your puppy to bark and yelp. Of course, it should be able to announce its presence, but if it goes on barking it must be called to order with a strict 'Quiet!'. If a puppy fails to obey, just hold its muzzle closed with your hand.

A dog will sometimes bark for long periods when left alone. It feels threatened and tries to get someone's attention by barking. There are special training programmes for this problem, where dogs learn that being alone is nothing to be afraid of, and that its master will always return.

You can practice this with your dog at home. Leave the room and come back in at once. Reward your dog if it stays quiet. Gradually increase the length of your absences and keep rewarding it as long as it remains quiet. Never punish the dog if it does bark or yelp. It will never understand punishment afterwards, and this will only make the problem worse. Never go back into the room as long as your dog is barking, as it will view this as a reward. You might want to make the dog feel more comfortable by switching the radio on for company during your absence. It will eventually learn that you always come back and the barking will reduce. If you don't get the required result, attend an obedience course.

Breeding

Dogs, and thus Cavaliers, follow their instincts, and reproduction is one of nature's important processes. For people who enjoy breeding dogs this is a positive circumstance.

For people who enjoy breeding dogs this is a positive circumstance. Those who simply want a cosy companion' however, do not need the regular adventures with females on heat and unrestrainable. Knowing a little about breeding in dogs will help you to understand why they behave the way they do, and the measures you need to take when this happens.

Liability
Breeding dogs is much more than simply 1+1= many. If you're planning to breed with your Cavalier, be on your guard, otherwise the whole affair can turn into a financial drama because, under the law, a breeder is liable for the 'quality' of his puppies.
The breeder clubs place strict conditions on animals used for bre-

ding. They must be examined for possible congenital defects (see the chapter Your Cavalier's health). This is the breeder's first obligation, and if you breed a litter and sell the puppies without these checks having been made, you can be held liable by the new owners for any costs arising from any inherited defects. These (veterinary) costs can be enormous! So contact the breed association if you plan to breed a litter of Cavaliers.

The female in season
Bitches become sexually mature at about eight to twelve months. Then they go into season for the first time. They are 'on heat' for two to three weeks. During this period they discharge little drops of blood and they are very

attractive to males. The bitch is fertile during the second half of her season, and will accept a male to mate. The best time for mating is then between the ninth and thirteenth day of her season. A female's first season is often shorter and less severe than those that follow. If you do want to breed with your female you must allow this first (and sometimes the second) season to pass. Most bitches go into season twice per year. If you do plan to breed with your Cavalier in the future, then sterilisation is not an option to prevent unwanted offspring. A temporary solution is a contraceptive injection, although this is controversial because of side effects such as womb infections.

Phantom pregnancy

A phantom pregnancy is a common occurrence with Cavaliers. The female behaves as if she has a litter. She takes all kinds of things to her basket and treats them like puppies. Her milk teats swell and sometimes milk is actually produced. The female will sometimes behave aggressively towards people or other animals, as if she is defending her young. Phantom pregnancies usually begin two months after a season and can last a number of weeks. If it happens to a bitch once, it will often then occur after every season. If she suffers under it, sterilisation is the best solution, because continual phantom pregnancies increase the

risk of womb or teat conditions. In the short term a hormone treatment is worth trying, perhaps also homeopathic medicines. Camphor spirit can give relief when teats are heavily swollen, but rubbing the teats with ice or a cold cloth (moisten and freeze) can also help relieve the pain. Feed the female less than usual, and makes sure she gets enough attention and extra exercise.

Preparing to breed

If you do plan to breed a litter of puppies, you must first wait for your female to be physically and mentally full-grown. In any event you must let her first season pass. To mate a bitch, you need a male. You could simply let her out on the street and she will quickly return home pregnant. But if you have a pure-bred Cavalier, then it certainly makes sense to mate her with the best possible candidate, even if she has no pedigree. Proceed with caution and think especially about the following: Accompanying a bitch through pregnancy, birth and the first eight to twelve weeks afterwards is a time consuming affair. Never breed with Cavalier that have congenital defects, and this also applies to dogs without papers. The same goes for hyperactive, nervous and shy dogs. If your Cavalier does have a pedigree, then mate her with a dog that also has one. For more information, contact the breed association.

Pregnancy

It's often difficult to tell at first when a bitch is pregnant. Only after about four weeks can you feel the pups in her womb. She will now slowly get fatter and her behaviour will usually change. Her teats will swell during the last few weeks of pregnancy. The average pregnancy lasts 63 days, and costs her a lot of energy. In the beginning she is fed her normal amount of food, but her nutritional needs increase in jumps during the second half of the pregnancy. Give her approximately fifteen percent more food each week from the fifth week on. The mother-to-be needs extra energy and proteins during this phase of her pregnancy. During the last weeks you can give her a concentrated food, rich in energy, such as dry puppy food. Divide this into several small portions per day, because she can no longer deal with large portions of food. Towards the end of the pregnancy, her energy needs can easily be one-and-a-half times more than usual.

After about seven weeks the mother will start to demonstrate nesting behaviour and starts to look for a place to give birth to her young. This might be her own basket or a special birthing box. This must be ready at least a week before the birth to give the mother time to get used to it. The basket or box should preferably be in a quiet place.

The birth
The average litter is three or four puppies. The birth usually passes without problems. Of course, you must contact your vet immediately if you suspect a problem!

Suckling
After birth, the mother starts to produce milk. The suckling period is very demanding. During the first three to four weeks the pups rely entirely on their mother's milk. During this time she needs extra food and fluids. This can be up to three or four times the normal amount. If she's producing too little milk, you can give both mother and her young special puppy milk. Here too, divide the high quantity of food the mother needs over several smaller portions. Again, choose a concentrated, high-energy, food and give her plenty of fresh drinking water, but not cow's milk, which can cause diarrhoea.

You can give the puppies some supplemental solid food when they are three to four weeks old. There are special puppy foods available that follow on well from the mother's milk and can easily

be eaten with their milk teeth. Ideally, the puppies are fully weaned off, at an age of six or seven weeks i.e. they no longer drink their mother's milk. The mother's milk production gradually stops and her food needs also drop. Within a couple of weeks after weaning, the mother should again be getting the same amount of food as before the pregnancy.

Castration and sterilisation
As soon as you are sure your bitch should never bear a (new) litter, a sterilisation is the best solution. During sterilisation the uterus is removed in an operation. The bitch no longer goes into season and can never become pregnant. The best age for a sterilisation is about eighteen months, when the bitch is more or less fully-grown.

A male dog is usually only castrated for medical reasons or to correct undesirable sexual behaviour. During a castration the testicles are removed, which is a simple procedure and usually without complications. There is no special age for castration but, where possible, wait until the dog is fully-grown. Vasectomy is sufficient where it's only a case of making the dog infertile. In this case the dog keeps its sexual drive but can no longer reproduce.

Sports and shows

Visiting a dog show is a special experience for both dog and master.

For some dog-lovers it is an intensive hobby, they visit countless shows every year. Others find it nice to visit an exemption show with their dog just once. It's worth making the effort to visit an exemption show where a judge's trained eyes will inspect your Cavalier and assess it for form, gait, condition and type. The judge's report will teach you your dog's weak and strong points, which may help you when choosing a mate for breeding. You can also exchange experiences with other Cavalier owners. Official exemption shows are only open to dogs with a recognised pedigree.

Ring training and club events
If you've never been to a dog show, you will probably be fumbling in the dark in terms of what will be expected of you and your dog. Many Cavaliers and general dog clubs organise so-called ring training courses for dogs going to a show for the first time. This training teaches you exactly what the judge will be looking for, and you can practice this together with your dog.

Open shows
All dog clubs organise dog shows. You must enter your dog in advance in a certain class. These metings are usually small and friendly and are often the first acquaintance dog and master makes with a "real" judge. This is an overwhelming experience for your dog - a lot of its contemporaries and a strange man or woman who fiddles around with it and peers into its mouth. After a few times, your dog will know exactly what's

expected of it and will happily go to the next club match.

Championship shows

Various championship shows take place during the course of the year with different prizes. These shows are much more strictly organised than club matches. Your dog must be registered in a certain class in advance and it will then be listed in a catalogue. On the day itself, the dog is usually kept on a bench until its turn comes up. During the judging in the ring, it's important that you show your dog at its best. The judge examines each dog in turn. When all the dogs from that class have been judged, the best are selected and placed. After all the judging for is finished all the winners of the various classes in that sex they compete for the Challenge Certificate in that sex. (3 Challenge certificates from different judges, and your Cavalier will be a Champion in the UK.) The best Cavalier in the eyes of the judge gets this award. Finally, the winners of each sex compete for the title of Best in Show.

Of course, your dog must look very smart for the show. The judge will not be impressed if its coat is not clean or is tangled, and its paws are dirty. Nails must be clipped and teeth free of plaque. The dog must also be free of parasites and ailments. A bitch must not be in season and a male must be in possession of both testicles.

Apart from those things, judges also hate badly brought-up, anxious or nervous dogs. Get in touch with your local dog club or the breed association if you want to know more about shows.

Don't forget!

If you're planning to take your dog to a club match or show, you need to be well prepared. Don't forget the following:

For yourself:

- Show documents if they have been sent to you
- Food and drink
- Clip for the catalogue number
- Chairs if an outside show

For your dog:
- Food and water bowls and food
- Dog blanket and perhaps a cushion
- Show lead
- A brush
- A benching chain and collar

Parasites

All dogs are vulnerable to various sorts of parasite. Parasites are tiny creatures that live at the expense of another animal.

They feed on blood, skin and other body substances. There are two main types. Internal parasites live within their host animal's body (tapeworm and round-worm) and external parasites live on the animals exterior, usually in its coat (fleas and ticks), but also in its ears (ear mite).

Fleas

Fleas

Fleas feed on a dog's blood. They cause not only itching and skin problems, but can also carry infections such as tapeworm. In large numbers they can cause anaemia and dogs can also become allergic to a flea's saliva, which can cause serious skin conditions. So it's important to treat dog for fleas as effectively as possible, not just on the dog itself but also in its surroundings.

For treatment on the animal, there are various medicines: drops for the neck and to put it in its food, flea collars, long-life sprays and flea powders. There are various sprays in pet shops that can be used to eradicate fleas in the dog's immediate surroundings. Choose a spray that kills both adult fleas and their larvae. If your dog goes in your car, you should spray that too.

Fleas can also affect other pets, so you should treat those too. When spraying a room, cover any aquarium or fishbowl. If the spray reaches the water, it can be fatal for your fish!

Your vet and pet shop have a wide range of flea treatments and can advise you on the subject.

Ticks

Ticks are small, spider-like parasites. They feed on the blood of the animal or person they've settled on. A tick looks like a tiny, grey-coloured leather bag with eight feet. When it has sucked itself full, it can easily be five to ten times its own size and is darker in colour.

Dogs usually fall victim to ticks in bushes, woods or long grass. Ticks cause not only irritation by their blood sucking but can also carry a number of serious diseases. This applies especially to the Mediterranean countries, which can be infested with blood parasites. In our country these diseases are fortunately less common. But Lymes disease, which can also affect humans, has reached our shores. Your vet can prescribe a special treatment if you're planning to take your dog to southern Europe. It is important to fight ticks as effectively as possible. Check your dog regularly, especially when its been running free in woods and bushes. It can also wear an anti-tick collar.

Ticks

Removing a tick is simple using a tick pincette. Grip the tick with the pincette, as close to the dog's skin as possible and carefully pull it out. You can also grip the tick between your fingers and, using a turning movement, pull it carefully out. You must disinfect the spot where the tick was using iodine to prevent infection. Never soak the tick in alcohol, ether or oil. In a shock reaction the tick may discharge the infected contents of its stomach into the dog's skin.

Cheyletiella Mite

Mites are just like tiny spider-like parasites. The Cavalier is often afflicted by infection with the Chelyetiella-Yasguri mite, also called scale mite or cat mite. Puppies and animals with reduced resistance are very vulnerable. The skin often shows dandruff (scales of skin) caused by the mites 'digging'. This can be accompanied by severe itching and hair loss. This beast can be easily fought off with an anti-parasite shampoo from your vets. Don't forget to treat the surroundings too, because this particular mite is very thick-skinned. Some people are also sensitive to this mite, and react with itching, small swellings and rashes. After treating your dog, take a shower and cream yourself on any itchy spots. Take care for any housemates who suffer from asthmatic conditions or allergies.

Worms

Dogs can suffer from various types of worm, The most common are tapeworm and roundworm. Tapeworm causes diarrhoea and poor condition. With a tapeworm infection you can sometimes find small pieces of the worm around the dog's anus or on its bed. In this case, the dog must be wormed. You should also check your dog for fleas, which carry the tapeworm infection.

Roundworm is a condition that reoccurs regularly. Puppies are often infected by their mother's milk. Your vet has medicines to prevent this. Roundworm causes problems (particularly in younger dogs), such as diarrhoea, loss of weight and stagnated growth. In serious cases the pup becomes thin, but with a swollen belly. It may vomit and you can then see the worms in its vomit. They are spaghetti-like tendrils.
A puppy must be treated regularly for worms with a worm treatment. Adult dogs should be treated every six months.

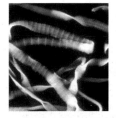

Worms

Your Cavalier's health

The space in this small book is too limited to go into all the Cavalier's medical ups and downs.

However, we do want to give some attention to a few diseases and anomalies that are more common to the breed. It is also useful to know that some Cavaliers can 'snore' when wound up, which some people wrongly call hyperventilation. Officially, the phenomenon is called "sneezing reverse" and is caused by the normal-length palate in its shortened snout. As soon as the dog swallows, the problem goes away. Many people grip their dog's snout to quickly eliminate this somewhat distressing situation.

Heart abnormalities
Abnormalities are usually to be found in the heart valves. The tissue around the valves degenerates, whereby the valve doesn't close properly. The tissue quality is no longer enough to meet the requirements for normal heart-valve functioning. The consequent leakage causes coughing and sometimes very serious distress due to lung blockages or lung oedema. The dog's endurance is reduced, it becomes abnormally tired (initially only after exercise, later even at rest), it loses its appetite and becomes thin. With the Cavalier, mitral prolapse and mitral insufficiency are often encountered at a much younger age than normal (around four or five years of age). It seems to be hereditary, but the precise cause is still unknown. Treatment by a vet is often necessary. This is an incurable progressive disease that progresses at widely different speeds (from a few months to eight or nine years). Giving medication after

heart problems are noticed prolongs the life and relieves the symptoms.

Patella Luxation

With this disorder, the kneecap does not sit properly on the end of the lower leg. The kneecap dislocates beside the joint. A luxated kneecap can be caused by a grove that is too shallow, which is hereditary, but also by a trauma (accident). In this case the luxation may be coupled with torn ligaments. Luxations can occur in various grades. The amount of difficulty and pain the dog suffers differs from one dog to the other.

Luxated kneecaps can be operated on. Just as with larger breeds, smooth floors and unusual movements (chasing a bouncing ball, hopping and turning) are not good for the joints of smaller breeds and puppies.

Progressive Retina Atrophy (PRA)

PRA is a degeneration of the retina that inevitably leads to blindness. In the early stages, the dog will still be able to see well in daylight until it's about five years old. However the condition leads to complete blindness between the dog's fifth and ninth year.

Cataracts

Checks for cataracts are made at the same time as the checks for PRA. This condition causes a clouding of the retina. It can appear in young animals and is passed on by both parents. If only a part of the retina is affected cataracts need not lead to total blindness, but unfortunately this is the consequence in most cases.

Entropion and ectropion

These are genetic conditions affecting the eyelids. With entropion the eyelids are curled inwards, with ectropion outwards. Both cause the eyelashes to lay on the eyeball causing irritation, which leads to red, watering eyes. The eyes become infected and discharge pus. This can cause serious damage to the cornea and

eventually even cause blindness. Entropion and ectropion can be corrected surgically.

Distichiasis

One or more rows of hairs that come out of the lower eyelid edge. These hairs irritate the cornea and, in the worst case, cause serious damage. This abnormality is hereditary, but fortunately can be surgically corrected.

Atresia punta lacrimalis (Atresia of the Eye)

In-born abnormality of the tear ducts. Here, the tears run over the edge of the eye-lid causing tear stripes. It is an hereditary defect that can be treated surgically, but the results are not always successful.

Tips for the Cavalier King Charles Spaniel

- A Cavalier is a soft-natured dog that won't respond well to a harsh hand.
- Ignore submissive or anxious behaviour; certainly don't comfort your dog.
- A Cavalier can be somewhat cocky; a rigorous, but not harsh, up-bringing is very important!
- Attend a puppy course with your dog. You'll both learn a thing or two.
- Visit several breeders before you buy a puppy.
- The Cavalier is an energetic dog. It will find dog sports great fun, but don't take them too seriously!
- It's first car journey is quite an experience for your puppy. Make sure it's a pleasant one.
- Check your Cavalier's coat for tangles regularly.
- Don't only fight fleas, but also the larvae.
- Taking your dog on vacation? Why not!
- Hard chunks and enough to chew on keep your dog's teeth healthy.
- Never buy a puppy if you weren't able to see its mother.
- Clean your dog's eyes each day.
- A puppy is a lot of work, and can cause grey hair.
- Buy a Cavalier via the breed association.
- Make sure your dog doesn't get too fat. Not too much to eat and plenty of exercise is the golden rule.

The Cavalier King Charles Spaniel on the internet

A great deal of information can be found on the internet. A selection of websites with interesting details and links to other sites and pages is listed here. Sometimes pages move to another site or address. You can find more sites by using the available searchmachines.

www.thecavalierclub.co.uk
The Cavalier King Charles Spaniel Club.

www.cavaliers.co.uk
This site provides information to Cavalier King Charles Spaniel owners and prospective owners interested in the breed either for Showing or Breeding as reflected in the United Kingdom.

www.cavalierkingcharles.com
Learn about your Cavaliers' care and wellbeing; discover their history, look up bibliographies, Cavalier clubs, and other websites and resources and more.

www.the-kennel-club.org.uk
The Kennel Club's primary objective is to promote in every way, the general improvement of dogs. This site aims to provide you with information you may need to be a responsible pet owner and to help you keep your dog happy, safe and content.

www.k9-care.co.uk
The Self-Help site for dog owners. A beautiful website with tons of information on dogs. All you need to know about grooming, training, health care, buying a dog, travel and much more.

www.thedogscene.com/index.htm
The Dog Scene, this site is dedicated to pedigree dogs in the United Kingdom. Dog breeds, articles and shopping mall are a number of the issues you can find on this website.

www.pet-insurance-uk.me.uk
Find low cost pet insurance via this UK pet insurance directory.

www.pethealthcare.co.uk
At pethealthcare.co.uk they believe that a healthy pet is a happy pet. Which is why they've brought together leading experts to create a comprehensive online source of pet care information.

www.onlinepetcare.co.uk
www.onlinepetcare.co.uk was launched in 2001 and contains information about and links to businesses and charities in the midlands area involved in the care and purchasing of domestic animals.

http://dogtraining.co.uk
Your central resource for dog-training, boarding kennels & vets in the UK.

www.k9magazine.com
This refreshing magazine is produced with today's conscientious dog owner in mind and provides a fascinating insight into the latest news, views and gossip from the UK and world dog scene as well as an easy access point to valuable advice, tips and expert opinion from some of the pet world's leading authorities.

www.rspca.org.uk
The Royal Society for the prevention of cruelty to animals. If you are interested in re-homing a dog (or other animal), pay a visit to your local RSPCA animal center. This site provides information on animal care.

www.ourdogs.co.uk
A website where you can find a variety of information on breeders, health issues, show calendar, competitions, general information on dogs and an online shop.

www.mypetstop.com
An international, multilingual website with information on keeping, breeding, behavior, health related issues and much more.

www.waltham.com
Waltham is a firm specialized in pet care and nutrition. On this website you can find more information on pet care, training and diets.

www.aboutpets.info
The website of the publisher of the About Pets book series. An overview of the titles, availability in which languages and where in the world the books are sold.

Breeder Clubs

Becoming a member of a breeder club can be very useful for good advice and interesting activities. Contac the Kennel Club in case addresses or telephone-numbers are changed.

Cavalier King Charles Spaniel Club
Sec. Mrs A Jones
Tel: 01490 430554

Eastern Counties Cavalier King Charles Spaniel Society
Sec. Ms M Hogan
Tel: 01462 670774

Humberside Cavalier King Charles Spaniel Club
Sec. Mrs R Mochrie
Tel: 01785 253717
Hillcrest Hopton Staffs st18 0AH
website www.cavaliers.co.uk
email editor@cavaliers.co.uk

Midland Cavalier King Charles Spaniel Club
Sec. Mrs M Rees
Tel: 01203 403583

West of England Cavalier King Charles Spaniel Club
Sec. Mr J Evans
Tel: 01453 822599

Northern Cavalier King Charles Spaniel Society
Sec. Mr I Sidgwick
Tel: 01228 561 209

Northern Ireland Cavalier King Charles Spaniel Club
Sec. Miss finlay
Tel: 028 90 851333

Scottish Cavalier King Charles Spaniel Club
Sec. Mrs l Gow
Tel: 0131 3392503

South & West Wales Cavalier King Charles Spaniel Club
Sec. Mr a close
Tel: 01446 737733

Southern Cavalier King Charles Spaniel Club
Sec mr g ford
Tel: 01962 772025

Other books from About Pets

- The Boxer
- The Border Collie
- The Cocker Spaniel
- The Dalmatian
- The Dobermann
- The German Shepherd
- The Golden Retriever
- The Jack Russell Terrier
- The Labrador Retriever
- The Puppy
- The Rottweiler
- The Budgerigar
- The Canary
- The Cockatiel
- The Parrot
- The Lovebird
- The Cat
- The Kitten
- The Dwarf Hamster
- The Dwarf Rabbit
- The Ferret
- The Gerbil
- The Guinea Pig
- The Hamster
- The Mouse
- The Rabbit
- The Rat
- The Goldfish
- The Tropical Fish
- The Snake

Key features of the series are:
- Most affordable books
- Packed with hands-on information
- Well written by experts
- Easy to understand language
- Full colour original photography
- 70 to 110 photos
- All one needs to know to care well for their pet
- Trusted authors, veterinary consultants, breed and species expert authorities
- Appropriate for first time pet owners
- Interesting detailed information for pet professionals
- Title range includes books for advanced pet owners and breeders
- Includes useful addresses, veterinary data, breed standards.

The Cavalier King Charles Spaniel

Name:	Cavalier King Charles Spaniel
FCI-classification:	Toy dogs (Group 9, section 8)
First standard:	Crufts 1928 (Great Britain)
Origin:	Great Britain
Original tasks:	Toy dog / hunting dog
Weight:	5.5 – 8 kg
Average life expectancy:	Approx. 10 years